Titles by *Langaa* RPCIG

T0198536

Letters to Marion

(And the Coming Generations)

Poems by

John Nkemngong Nkengasong

Langaa Research & Publishing CIG
Mankon, Bamenda

Publisher:
Langaa RPCIG
(Langaa Research & Publishing Common Initiative Group)
P.O. Box 902 Mankon
Bamenda
North West Province
Cameroon
Langaagrp@gmail.com
www.langaapublisher.com

Distributed outside N. America by African Books Collective
orders@africanbookscollective.com
www.africanbookscollective.com

Distributed in N. America by Michigan State University
Press
msupress@msu.edu
www.msupress.msu.edu

ISBN: 9956-558-65-6

DISCLAIMER

This is a work of fiction. Names, characters, places, and incidents are either the author's invention or they are used fictitiously. Any resemblance to actual places and persons, living or dead, events, or locales is coincidental.

Dedication

For
my daughter

Marion

Contents

Preface

Writing poetry is an obsession not just in the simplistic sense that the poet communicates his mind in the most profound and sincere manner. Each poem is a milestone on the poet's journey through the past and a signpost on his journey into the future. The crafted word thus becomes a symbol of the most valued of values and communicates not just feelings as Wordsworth intimated but it seeks also to produce ideas that are invaluable for the positive construction of the society as the poet walks through life. Accordingly, the poet is not a mere singer of mellifluous verse but a legislator, a searcher and preserver of the Truth, and a provider of alternative visions for the future.

My passion for poetry developed early in my secondary school days after reading poets like John Milton and William Shakespeare whose works fascinated me with the grandeur of their expression and the revelation of profound feelings and noble ideas. Thus the first poem I ever wrote titled "Five Years Begun, Five Years Ended" which was published in the Seat of Wisdom College magazine, *Wisdom Vigil,* was written after a pattern derived especially from Milton. Apart from the title of the poem which I have modified in the present collection and which now reads "The Beginning", I have hardly found a reason to alter its original structure and content. I have always considered the poem to be the symbol of my creative imagination because my earlier vision of the world recorded in the poem permitted me to penetrate other realms of experience in a much mature and varied manner as I expressed in the later poems and other genres. It set the pace for a creative venture which has remained an obsession throughout my life.

While it may be said that the grandeur of poetry lies to a major extent in its esoteric contemplations, I did not find it immediately accessible in addressing some expedient issues in contemporary experience. For a long time my passion for poetry seemed to have been shaken off by my involvement with other genres not necessarily because poetry was ineffective in expressing the ideas I had, but that contemporary experience has been so fluctuating that I needed, as I thought, a forum through which I could reach out to the audience with urgency. The Cameroonian experience in particular has been stifling, especially from 1990 when the country was saddled with a number of problems including the economic crises, political buffoonery, squandamania, and corruption which reached their apogee at the turn of the century.

However, I did not abandon poetry altogether. While venturing into drama and fiction, I still wrote some poetry taking into consideration its social, spiritual and metaphysical functions, and especially, its ability to provide contemplative clues to the prevailing circumstances. Some of the poems have been published in anthologies, magazines and journals. My apology to poetry is therefore inspired by the fact that I have not given to the time-honoured genre the highest esteem as it would have been my wish. The publication of this collection is consequently an attempt to reconcile the self with the art and to demonstrate, of course, that poetry remains the most noble of art given its power to explore the recesses of the imagination and come to terms with the hidden secrets of the universe.

A comprehensive collection of poems would normally provide clues to the periods within which the poems were written in order to enhance understanding of their contexts. While that is relevant to some extent, a poem may still enjoy the right to liberal existence. There is nevertheless an attempt in this collection to render the poems in the order in which they were written. For structural reasons however, the positions of some of the poems especially the longer ones have been altered to make reading more accessible. Whatever the value of the poems as independent units, or as having a liaison with contemporary experience, has to be judged by the reader who best determines the true tone, taste and spirit of poetry based on his/her valued judgments. For, a poet is never a good judge of his own works. He is only an agent of creativity through whom poetic matter is communicated and his major preoccupation is always whether or not he has succeeded in expressing the feelings and ideas that overflow the banks of his imagination.

John Nkemngong Nkengasong

The Coming of the Sages

The Manjong drums rumble
The coming of the sages
Carrying calabashes of knowledge
On their heads
From their wanderings far and wide
To the rolling hills of Nweh
Where valleys heap beyond valleys

Lightening flashes
In the womb of the thunderstorm
As Lebialem Falls roar down the cliff
And the rains pour from the lakes above
And the winds hoot their whistling horns
Through trees that bow
To the rhythm of the gong

To Fuandem, the young and the old,
Take your offerings of tethered rams,
Palm wine, colanuts and all
At the solemn shrine, stink
The air with herbs of sacrifices
As of old, stoop in supplication
And wake the long-forgotten god

Buièh tangtê mbo éééh....
And sing and dance as the sages come
With arty tales of ancient times
In your ordained wears
Strike the Manjong tunes and
Flog the drums till they bleed out melody
Weave the Akoh xylophones
While the women shake their bosoms in frenzy
And the men draw and clang their machetes
And seal the rhythm of ecstasy
In the rising dust
To ancestors in the underworld.

Spear and Shield

I lost my spear,
I lost my shield
When in my teens
The battle of the world
Was at its prime.
Where will I hide my head
in a searing world
When death shut him in the grave?

Many Julys since
I peep thro' the mousy mound
through the rotting boards
with sighs and salty tears
Where Asaba Nkemngong's
remnants lie...

the mungo

the anchored barges
on our shores, their carousing
sails in mournful westward winds
the hooting of an owl
an evil song in the thickets
a full ripe moon
its radiance in the ocean
(that widest road to slavery)

there was greed
in that madrush of howling waves
that auctioned me from my cradle

our quifons
for they stood resolute
and wore black caps and
red feathers, pulled the oars
for the slavers
swearing they'd drown the river mungo

2

till the land becomes one
and the people one

we were forsaken
in the thorn-strewn plantations
in those horizons where the sun
takes a midday meal, and returning
was dearer than our dear lives

our quifons
they emerged from the shade
chewing hard crumbs of bread
their voices dry
like the proverbial ants' and urged
our new masters on with whips
for our bodies
shackles for our necks

i cry
the zuluman's cry
that split south afrik's heart
i shed the widow's tears
that drowned all ireland
ha! the wicked blow
which ruined old harlem's ribs
i hear the accursed slave
sang misery to deaf white ears
as i sing now to deaf-black ones

they say
god was not awake when i was born
and the colour of a slave is black
and i must follow in my shackles
and till their soils round those horizons
where the sun takes its midday meal
i must follow gently, slavemasters
to your volitions until the mungo drowns
and the land becomes one.

The Princely Kite

So high he roams
the immense sky
flapping his imperial wings
on his mighty chest
and perches on the towers
of the blue

so high he sails in the sky
before a train of colourful clouds
to fair and foreign lands
where lies a pleasure
known to few

so high the great bird
searches far across the sky
and swoops down
on a little humble chick
and to the highest perch it flies

till death plays his timely trick
and down he flutters
the princely kite
like a leaf loose in the wind.

The Labours of a Boy

Many are the labours of a boy
If he wants to be a better man
He'll pass through life with joy
With as ample glory as he can.

Many are the sorrows of a lad
If an indolent life he had
He'll pass through life in tears
With acute misery of the years.

Little Chick

Little chick filing out
in a brood at dawn
chirping praises to the
new-born day
in furs of crystal,
soft and warm

Little chick strutting into
the glaring morning's snare
where the bird-prey
keeps a silent watch
on the cotton tree on the heath
you sucked the silent night

Little chick, so honest and so fair
did he that gave you life
frame the bitter clutches
of the kite and the unpitying
 jaws of greedy men

Stay, stay away at roost,
innocent bird
for the beautiful morn's full of lusts
than you can tell.

Song of a Convict

Listen to the weaver birds
Speaking treason in the wind
Nay, see the joyous fowls
In daggered plumages
Parleying at the royal gate
In blissful libertine

On towers where they roost
Hear them, hear them
Hear them quack

And twitter and chirp
Yet, no knight nor squire
To quote the law

Beneath that tree I sit
Manacled in censured frames
Storming life with sighs
And flooding tears away
Envying that liberty
Which man from man usurped.

Wailing in the Jungle

Will no one listen to the silent cries
From shanties choked with th'offending
    midnight breeze
The scythes of oppression whirling in the wind
And the venom of corruption searing
    in plebeian blood?

It's a cataclysm of terror and misery
With slaves in tyrants' garbs
    turned amuck
Turned rodents in the barns of fruitful
    motherland
Will no one listen to the cry of the humble?

No one listens to the tortured infant wail
No one hears its pitying mother's sigh
No one heeds to the old farm-farer's groan
    in the jungle

The Jugglers of the State are at banquet
Browsing in foreign laps
They will return like nabobs
After our little wells are drained
To water Europe's greener lawns

nevermore, Fuandem, nevermore
nevermore the milky dawns
at your shrine's shores
the rhythm of your gong is drowned
and the waters of mighty Mungo dry
and want of drink, the humble's cry
and life is death
and death is life
in my blind and bitter fatherland.

The Ballot-Box

Some codger came to me
down the road
carrying an only ballot-box
singing praises to democracy

I said to him:
Let the wild nut sink its roots
where the soil is moist
a lichen may choose a rock
or the bark of a tree
and if a duck lay in a cobra's mouth
let it be its will and free...

Franchise Manager, pass on
a tornado has swept my little store
and I have no grains
to sow in the Sahara.

The Slaughter House

I hear the bleat of lambs
in the plundering cities
as the cannons boom
their enchanting songs

their fiery blazing
tears the midnight care
and spears wheeze a
moan-like moan questioning
hearts that were pure

the wolves are tearing
into the fold again
the lamb's neck pressed
against poignant swords to admit
what they know not
of a slave turned tyrant

the African dawn is blood
spilt over handsome
negroid pastures
with corpses coughing blood
the boon of a
chilly night's industry
of the imperial race
and the black slave turned amuck
groping for the heights of Africa.

Africa, My Africa

When in the heart of night
I hear the rifles
bang their mortal songs
I know a tyrant has murdered sleep
as he gropes for the heights of Africa

our mornings wake in the mire
of blood
our lushful greens, littered
with lives that had known life

and our days recede
in fear
and misery, gnawed away
by hunger and disease....

Africa,
my Africa
when shall your children live
the unlived centuries of their ancestors?

Lysona

When the parrot's song ends
with roost on a twig
in the calm of the wilderness

when the red round moon
wanders unscarred
thro' his dominions

when the throttling snores
of tired folk
speak comfort in chambers
where they sleep

when little streams
grove the chests of river stones
and the bristling dew
naps on breasts of
night-veiled flowers

when the whistling lullaby
of the midnight breeze
and of the enchanter, the cricket
drowns me in the dream

I meet that face again
and the hybrid soul in her
that belonged to me.

A Coffin for Dr. Mbella Pe

Dr. Mbella Pe stood
by his hungry coffin
flanked by sour students
whose future bleak
they caught the Chancellor
to diagnose
and profess their ailing fates
before they buried him live

the grey man, unruffled stood
with marquis defiance
and bold temperance
like a ghost that haunts at noon
and chilled the flames of
the fluttering red candles burning
his *veritas hominis* on the coffin

Espion! Espion! went the cry
instantly, fierce soldiers
thudded in and out the scene
charging like overdrugged bulls
and tore the mob with
the wrath of monsters
a medley of panic
as multi-thousand youthful undertakers
of Dr. Mbella Pe fled for life

That day, their victim fell
more than three scores captured
the day before by valiant militiamen
in defence of the state...
a lad who had a day before spotted a spy
the drunken soldiers fell on him
pounding his jawbones to chaff
with rifle butts and batons
they grabbed his throat and off
they went bound for inferno
filled with pride and fulfilment
of capturing the Queen's Commander

Knowing what devils reigned
in the noxious underground cells
of the *vallée de la morte*
the lad feigned fainted
and his captors relaxed their hold
he found his feet and sped
down the Ngoa-kele slopes
like a maddened foe
before his oppressors caught
and murdered him
and make him tenant of a coffin
meant for the indifferent Dr. Mbella Pe

a clatter of rifles and thudding boots
angry voices swearing as they chased
Arrêtez le! Arrêtez l'Anglo!
Elément subversif!
if a bullet got his head...
but he vanished in the thickets
of panicking students
choking and coughing blood
uttering spongy words of woe
out of battered jawbones
a hard way
to be an undergraduate
Sapienta Collativa Cogito!

Unrequited

O heart, broken heart
batter yourself
and batter this frail frame too
I have pined
in the drudgery of the world
one thousand centuries gone
till the dam was cleared
and fresh water poured
had I the turn to snatch
my breath from decayed love
now my heart is tied to a rock

being for her sake
had I seized my head
and dashed it in the lion's mouth
live beheaded like
a stump in the desert
and wink at a woman's smile...

O heart, broken heart
love unreturned is
a hot-baked bombshell
in a human heart.

On the Toilet

I come, Invisible Presence
to your shrine
in obeisance to your call
bowel crammed
mind blistered
with fevers from the world.

Squatted in the marble sanctuary
consumed in a ritual of purgation
of self and soul
eyelids closed
against the door to battered life
and amidst the fretful fart
and gleeful groans
dream piles upon dream

dream piles upon dream
till self and soul resume
a dialogue
and lines of verse
come dancing in my eye
singing songs of PEACE and BLISS

Invisible Master Initiate
though I go from hence
chaste and pure
let the jolting lines of verse
sojourn
so I can spread
your precious gift
in the eyes of the world.

M'mendi

M'mendi, Mother Procreatess
sacred womb of million progenies
like the pregnant fish
in the corner of a lake
one million years ago

your progeny tied men's hearts
to her stakes with strings
and crushed them under
the wheels of fatal love
planted thorns in their minds
till men cried loud
and woke God in His sleep

she came from your soul
this hot-cold-blooded being
the prized artefact of your dream
you clothed her in silk and thorns
spiced her tongue
with honey and bile
fed her with milk and venom

Mother Procreatess
what lovable symmetry
is the queen of your womb
what vile empress is her gorgon soul
I caressed her silk
got pricked by thorns

kissed her tongue, tasted of the bile
drank her milk and poison
has deadened my nerves

M'mendi, Mother Procreatess
what labyrinth is your womb?

Cameroon

Is this the lusty Fatherland
my ancestors sang in song
whose fountains flowed
with honey and milk
and her green fields
pulsed like a wanton maiden's breast?

is this the bustling realm
her valleys strewn with velvet gold
her plains, a bed of crimson love
rolling mountains
rugged with leopards' skins
and towering forests
spread with magic fruits
like the garden of the gods
and the whispering rivers flooding
into enchanting seas?

is this the cradle of my life
haven of ancestral love
whose spirits guarded men
and cared for men in the sacrificial rite
when the ram danced to the tone
of its gurgling blood?

this is my country, Cameroon!
her skies drabbed in nimbus garbs
her song, the splitting thunder in the storm
her laughter, the cry of hungry children

because bastards risen from a dream
under neo-colonial canopies
have brought death into our lives

this is my country, Cameroon
I can't feel her warmth any more
God alone knows
I can't feel her warmth any more.

The Lament of a Youth

I am alone
on the harrowing path
crouched
between rude fangs of life
crushed
and munched like boneless viands

here
in the adamant fists of fate
in a little world
too large with pain
too sore with crime

here
in the lake of tears
no sunny day lit a face
but everyday
gush silent rivers
sailing down the cheeks
as their excellencies
will not let me thrive

inflicted drops
O gloom
righteous and forsaken
in life without essence
I tremble like the reed
on the banks of Cold Sea.

Song of a Lunatic

I live in the years
searing and serene
I live the scalding years
baneful like the barren sucker
crumbling in
the breath of wind

I have been a desert
and wandered through
my shrubless self
under the wrath of the sun

I have been a snail
that since that primal dawn
trailed into the deep forest
but never reached
its journey's end

I have been the quarry
and the quarryman
breaking the stones
in the core of my heart

I still break stone
my head's grown bald
with scratching
my mouth gaped with yawning
grown tired like years...
the years that come and go.

On Delirium

They're are cast away
by the vanity of men
to seek death in life
on refuse heaps
because their tongues are barbarous
and their ways are wild
like the wild birds of the sky

they are not wise, they are not rich
salacred on junks of sane waste
cursed by thinking men
to gnaw their dung
and drink their filth
and live like beggarly children
of the universe
flies nibbling their bodies
like vultures would
beck the carcass of a dying ass

yet we are all men
who on our first day
walked naked on the shores of life
tottering like young apes
making friends with dirt

we are all men
bitter with the insanity
of passion and ambition
we are all men
toiling after death's dark desire
we are all men
clung to the faltering claim
of wisdom, logic and reason
we are all mad men
chasing civilisation like
children tracking their own shadows

But where is their fate
this undying generations on the heap
squawking and dancing
smiling lonely
far away from life
of rational men
so chaste and peaceful in the mind

wrapped in unfettered worlds
they climb the imagination
rung by rung
till they reach God's home

this undying generations on the heap
they are diviners
pass them quietly
because you wake them from the dream.

Infatuation

Undo the manacles
of infatuation
stupid little cud
and sing
the clock bird's song
Eve could not see the sun
with a lidless eye
no woman shall
and Adam falls.

Dalila's Napkins

Since that day
she woke from sleep
under Adam's greasy loins
and blinded Samson's innocence
taught old French Louis
how to melt an empire on her lips

since that day
the world pulsed with the
pulsing dream of life
and life made death
and blistered hope
on the lipstick of a dame
and on her sheets

no mind can 'scape
Dalila's curse
or her bantered commercial shame...

those Eden blackened eyes
unremitting in their passions
who has seen them light
seen them light on dreams
nay, swoop paradise into
one terrible night of horror?

The Magus I
(For Mbella Sone Dipoko)

Beware
enchanting magus from the West
who brought to our world
offerings flickering with life
when we lay caput
in the grey corridors of death

But
someone has hid a canker
in his dream and eclipsed our world
from the brightly skies.

Though,
priest picaresque
he stands by his people's faltering hope
he stands too
on their graves greasiest edge
from within an infernal politic den.

For,
those fiendish midgets, who can tell?
when their dark
politic hour's dawn,
they'd prick his sight
for seeing so plain.

Beware
secret seer sublime
bequeath the ballot and the box to men
and turn the wick
turn higher the wick
you, light beyond life.

The Magus II
(For Mbella Sone Dipoko)

Sango!
For long, you hid a canker
in your dream
when fresh fruits were falling
from the tornadoes of an ancient century
and dulled that lamp
that led the blind
when our fate was dark
on the grey corridors of death

You too were Lord Mayor
from within an infernal politic den:
and sent violent winds
on treetops
whose leaves were shed.
In those days
your mouth was filled
with stale crumbs of bread
from their Majesty's putrid droppings
and you could not speak

Now I hear a vacuous mouth
sing honour in an empty song
of the scorching Mayor
Mbella Moki
no poet but bearer of the Truth

Sango,
while you stand between two rifts
I see your vision
turn all muddy in venereal Mungo
I hear its pelting voice
gurgle drowning words of wisdom
I hear it
deep in my aching heart.

Church Bells Summon

The distant tolls call
from their towers on the deserted hill
and my heart's filled with lead
at Crossroads
where I'm strayed
gazing the fires of deep dark hell
roar and devour
my vulnerable flesh.

I toddled on...
I toddled on
to the world that gave me breath
and could not return

The Holy Bells moan and
clang and weep
but I pace my way away
into a lotus jungle
into a wild honey forest
for baits which speak a world of beauty

Led to the heights of Fako Mounts
ushered into a treasured world
of lusts
from Babylonian towers
how could I return?

Nineteen Hundred and Ninety-one

Twenty centuries gyring to their end
have met kings auctioning thrones
the world speaks a common tongue
of freedom, peace and liberty
and the urn now wears the crown

one man in the land of prawns
put snuff in the wind

cleared thick heads
and a light gleamed on faces
that begot new civilisations

ah, John Fru Ndi!
you would not hear him
groan frothy politic words
you'd not see him walk by night
and plant thorns
on kinship path
can any one hurt that messiahman
and 'scape the voice of doom
a goliath who threw his heart
in a lion's mouth
and the carnivore ground her teeth to dust
who else could shield the clan
from the rolling rocks
with his only chest?

this is August Nineteen Ninety-one
the century's feet are running cold
the voices of doom are dying
and God's paradise its hour come at last
rounds up a sweep of a tortuous world.

To a Gecko on My Window Pane

Subtle beast
stare not too deep in my innocent heart
I know not what evil looms the threshold
from where you've taken sudden flight
and chilled my frozen mind

look not too deep in my soul
that now a tyrant's victim who
never danced the rhythm of its own song

I stayed away from Liberty Club last night
but something divulges my deeps of mind

derision besieges the neighbourhood
and I saw pestilence in a dream

for certain joy is bereaved and
the messengers of doom have reached our cities
their coarse voices speak out plain:
our wells are drained to water Europe's
greener lawns
as minions rage for Afrik's princely thrones
and they have gone behind the cloak of night
to plant woe under our feet.

On the Bamenda Massacre

A king is a mother's child
Yet how many hundred princes have kings
slain to clutch the crown
how many hundred mothers mourn
the blessings of their wombs
Ntarikon women's tears drop in my heart
their throaty shrieks sink my mind
nay, revoke that 26 May doomsday
when their wet eyelids, their swelled eyeballs
touched my nerves
but let them weep
till their infants' ghosts are raised
those nimbus drops make for brighter days
let them sigh
till their winds have rumpled palace walls
and nevermore will our mothers weep
nevermore will our women sigh
when Fuandem shall raise his head.

Ghost Towns

The burning roofs
the hooting of rifles
across the crowd
Nwofor is dead
blood oozing life into
thirsty graves
the cities cold
streets littered with lives
that had known life
and ghosts in macabre masks
have walked out of night
to haunt the day

on our streets
women walk naked
their children's blood
has ached their wombs
and Takembeng's fleshy groins
have dazed Essingan
flung lecherous potentates
out of sense

on our streets
hilarious violence greets
and street boys
have grabbed tyrant's garbs
and kings have gone in hiding
swearing God made the prince
and forged his crown

on our streets
the infant's cry breeds new fears
the smoking roofs
stir panting hearts
the crashing panes
the dark sires are a-haunting
the king's militia leaning on
gleaming butts are a-sighing.

Song To My Country People

O watchful stars, O guiding lamps
Lead my people through the cramps
Of doom's dark sinister corridors
Through freedom's boundless doors

We plough the fields we do not reap
Deprived of fortune stacked on the heap
My country's betiwrecked in vain
My country people gagged in betidrain

The awful night's dragged too long
We grind stone in mills with angry song
When our land's honey and milk rich
No haven in the world can reach

Countrymen, hang on testes of oppression
Till dizzy they faint in suppression
Tears, salty tears, drop in our hearts
Make them bitter till bastards dub their hats

Let them quarter us, maim and lacerate
Let them rage and swear and mutilate
But countrymen, hang on, in your doom
On our red blood, Cameroon will bloom.

A Tear for Siga Asanga

Si
ga
was
man
and
builder
of men
the Royal
Spear that
shot through
the heart of
tyranny

and Cameroon
breathed fresh and
savory life

Siga, death has made
you live for ever!

Mfoundi Faery

Sweet dame, sweet woman in her prime
You cannot see how stars gaze in wonder
That lovely bloom of yours
Till they are shaken out of wits
And the sun has taken sudden flight

Sweet woman symbol of god
You cannot know what anguish this hour bears
You cannot hear the clatter
And the clang of falling walls
The boom! boom! bang! of the rifles
And the wullillilliying of dying voices
For the Arch Artist stowed
His idol on holy ground
Far, far away from misery

Sweet woman, O blossom night
Your glossy laps have shamed the moon
And that lustre on your lips
Once withered the rose of tyranny
Your breath, that gentle morning breeze
Engendered life
And poets smiled like lunatics

Come to me, woman of my dream
And mould my rending heart
Come to me, woman of my soul
And give it respite from meditation
Come to me procurer of my soul
And haul me to your Eden, O bright Eternity!

And she came to me, vendor of my soul
And she came to me, woman of my doom
And she came to me, O dark eternity
No embittered soul broke the damp
Of salty sorrows as now I do
Knowing one thing: beauty wears daggers.

My Birthday Party

Thirty-three years above the earth
my heart clock ticks like
the senile sobs of a senior celibate

thirty-three unruffled years of the dream
slyly bar the gates of wanton youth
and unlatch the doors to un-stirring darkness

with one whore-kid and two grey hairs
a spurious fortune and a fatty dream
I've done naught, put no meaning in my life

a poor memory and a keen vision -
these blessings of my birth are stale
pregnant with prophesy, ink denies my flow

what shall I tell the world this day
having lived like a dry twig
in the currents of Lebialem Falls.

that like the Npkwe masquerade
I'll prance and fret on the arena
and never will be heard again

tarry, tarry, you hurrying feet of years
slow down, you giant paces of infirmity
till I've dressed my grave stone with immortal words.

Requiem for Lady of State

She's dead and gone, beloved Mother I...
Her soul buried in a coffin
Her body walks the night
In yonder forests of the South

No woman showed much tenderness
No heroine wept for a nation on its knees
Would she come again to soothe with bile
Now that she's dead and gone

She was the mirror of the state
Our gloom, on her painted lips could see
Beautiful when her fate was poor
Ugly when fortune made her rich

How dismal her lonely lunatic lover looks
Much grieved with so great loss
Of the better part of his heart
Husband or matador, who'd wipe his tears

Who'd soothe him in his dance of mourning feats
Chased naked by the wretched kids
Power clenched in his armpit, and the knife
That carnaged the sweetheart of the state

She will not come again, Lady of State
On the day before Christ is born
To throw on kids laced packets of plastic toys
Pampering the toys and not the sickly babes

She will not come again, loving Lady of State
With her mighty widow's mite to share
To infants drabbed in mortal ailment
To sneer at shrieking babes, touching none

She'll never come again, First Lady I....
Smiling with the wrong side of her mouth
Loving our beautiful cities, and oh!
Burning them all again with a fiery kiss

She's dead and gone, enchanting Lady I....
Her soul buried in a coffin
Her body walks the macabre night
In yonder forests of the South.

Essingan Dancers

Infernal rhythms
throbs of bleeding drums
beat in our ears
and, ruptured in a dance of terror
they shattered our dreams
like smashed skulls on the tarmac...
these gorgons masked in Mbeh Lekang
they passed us, one by one
in our mournful dusk chorusing:

    Lie, Commeniy, lie
    Till the devil
    Obeys your call

first was Terror, butcher and strangler
thousand corpses on a single face
each face crying its death, he edged on
swinging hatchet and matchet
and we died in horror
our nerves stifled like
the fibres of a dead coconut
as he sang the chorus:

    Lie, Commeniy, lie
    Till the devil
    Obeys your call

then came Pride
a modern man, modern thief
he danced, no devil had his match
this Essingan sorcerer
he wrapped our hopes in vanity
and swore by the axe
and a crown of thorns
no one'll pinch his crumb
while he lived
he followed the chorus singing

Lie, Commeniy, lie
Till the devil
Obeys your call

now a noble, Liar advanced
an awful mask, that unhorned fiend
the fanged adder cached in the green
swearing truth
biting the keen sword's edge
danced in the night and swore by day
no soul could see his feet
and I heard his voice:

I, Commeniy, lie
And the devil
Obeys my command.

Last came the Essingan master mask
he wore the head of an ancient ram
if you could neither see nor hear
you could smell ululations
if not, his lustful scent of a ram
frenzied in the rhythm of the dance
fretting like a beheaded ram
that set all a-giggling
in the village market square
he halted the rhythm at its peak to say:

Lie, Commeniy, lie
But I fear
You are devil and no liar.

Human Indignity

Nature made man supreme
over all things living and unliving
Man savoured her wealth
But he was lonely
and he wept and hid in the armpit of a rock
because he was lonely.
Nature said: "Do you, son, weep when
all things beautiful
in the Universe were meant
for your lone glory?
I made all these to keep you happy.
Most favoured of all creation
I gave you a tongue, reasoning and a soul
only you in the bestial universe
Why then do you weep
when all this is for your joy?"
Man said: "See how plentiful are the stars,
the birds and the honey-bees
each in its own kind flock together
but I'm alone."
Then Nature made a womb to multiply
and called it "woman."
From woman sprang progenies of million years
from the beginning of the universe.
Out of his bitter soul
man loathed, begrudged and slay his kin
to possess the things of the Universe
which Nature made free and beautiful,
abundant in the vales and on the plains
on the hills and in the rivers, in the air....
Now, when the coffin lid seals his eyes
And lowered six feet into maternal earth
man is lowlier than the earth worm
twining in the veins of the earth.

Letters to Marion (And the Coming Generations)

Ken Saro-Wiwa

Those that killed
Ken Saro-Wiwa

are now dead
and now

Ken Saro-Wiwa
he lives.

When I shall not Live

When one morning
I shall wake from sleep
To find that I have
Sailed to darkness
Let no tears flow
Like streams that lacked
valleys

Like the tears
Of a woman whose filthy bond
At court door
Strangled a buoyant life

No, let no one think
Of the pieces
Of broken hope
Deserted on the corridors
Of entangled visions
Of the nuptial bond.

To the Son of Mvoondoo

From Nkem Nkengasong
the Apostle of Truth
sojourned by Fuandem into the universe
to prophesy.

To the son of Mvoondoo
the sanctified sinner
and the ramified ram.

Glory and peace to all countrymen
by fatuous tyrannical arts afflicted;
greetings to you from the ancestors
and the gods, the spirits
and the potent of our clan.
I salute, also the boundless bounty
of Nature, the multi-coloured
plumaged birds, the antic seas
the trees, and stars...
all things living and unliving
that breathe in the womb of the universe.

Son of Mvoondoo,
seed of the rushing wind
for your Omni-impotence
these words are dressed
to soothe a seething mind,
knowing one thing:
I shall be felled in my grave
when your will is word.
Glory is he who like a pig
cries out plain, when a bawdy butcher
goes for the neck, for he shall not die
like sheep, saying nothing.
Therefore, these Truths,
I speak them free of charge
to mend a fractured heart.

I do not chide anyone, only Truth does.
For, I am man, vulnerable like men,
subjected to the word and will of Nature
Who and only who has a whip.
But if a leader must be beyond reproach
he must have a conscience,
belong to men and to the universe,
must have a family and manage it well,
must shriek if a bullet scathed a stone
on which we men feel our feet,
must sacrifice his life
for man's eternal glory
in Nature's timeless Universe.
The glory of life
is the generosity of Nature, and we men
must show compassion
to the things Nature created
because we are natural
and are to Nature bound.

Son of Mvoondoo,
you are the ram that led the shepherd
late to the village market.
In our misery,
we pulled you from behind
but you twisted the tether
and lay in the corner of a bush unruffled.
We put you to the lead
you dragged us towards a different road
and we arrived the feast at sunset.
We are the asses
on which you ride through all paradises
and make us trudge on our knees
like tired camels.
When we complain
you whip us on our skulls
with copper whips.

It has been said the
the tears of a people are the gods',
scrawled in a thousand books

how Frenchman Louis
fled naked across the Alps
from crumbling hellish bastilles.
And when King Dada ate human flesh
with wild pepper
slaves chased him
from his cherished throne
with a dish of adder's meat.
See prodigal Chief Bedel,
he asked for pardon
and procured a grave of thorns.
And your coughing progenitor,
El Hadj Amajou,
who sat in rank with Muhammad
who could tell him he was a man
governed by Nature?
This man, he died before his day!
and his corpse never has found a grave.
Who will go tell a Master Sergeant
in tyrannical arts
that Monrovia maimed a deity?
Ancestor Hoiphet, he dreamed
Methuselah blood filled his veins
and infirmity felled him in his grave
and falling he wept like a youth.

Son of Mvoondoo,
when the century's last rushing winds
creaked on rooftops
singing songs of Human Rights
did you not feel the cold?
Did you not hear the children cry
when the slayers your palace raised
stabbed our hearts
and robbed us of our lives
when strangers, like termites
eat the flanks of our fatherland?
Rigour and Moralisation...
what has wisdom said,
what has a wild ram done
bleating in tautened tether
and pulling the clan to your shambles?

37

We sniffed the poisoned air
and sneezed out life.
Our mornings woke on dead grassfields
the traitors had their waning silver coins.
Our lives auctioned
our corpses mortgaged,
we children of the clan
crave till our bellies are levelled
with our spinal cords.
What witchcraft?
See how cranky we have become.
See how bereft is our fate.
We swam in our burgeoning seas
till you drained it all
to cool a whoreson's scorching heart.
Go, sheep, uncomplaining!
Go unheard to your slaughter-house.
Go and grace Muhammadan feasts
and the children's blood rock your brain.

Son of Mvoondoo,
you are no shepherd, you are a ram;
you are no tyrant, democrat, none;
Though a tyrant maims and lacerates,
he has his laws and a line of thought.
And a democrat, if he must thrive,
he must be a wise, intelligent man, for
he confronts wiser, stupider men, being man.
Son of Mvoodoo, you are none
but a rogue fleeing God's wrath,
holy sugar caved in the armpit of your soul...
You are the ram that twists
the fates of men, stubborn
senseless, without predictions,
and now our lot is darker than your mind.
Go, ram beheaded, to the feasts;
go serve Mohammadan dish....

All men wear not a single crown,
all men plough not the fields,
all men weave not cloth.

That's why we found a man
chosen among men by men
to vouchsafe peace and glory among men
because we are many like the stars
and our minds and desires
vary like all things living and unliving
which Nature begot.
You, son of Mvoondoo
turned the ballot-box up-side-down
and trampled on our hopes in the mire.

Leadership is the call of Nature
but a ram is the call of the feasts.
The croaky voice of a burglar saint
and shepherd of men thereafter
is like the idiot gnawing
rotten flesh on the rubbish heap.

Son of Mvoondoo, here is the word:
Truth is the primal law of Nature
no man, however great, can warp it.
The righteous live by Truth
and not by the sword
and sly politic-words
or healthy pockets of chinks.
We men must know
we toil after death's dark desire.
We are all children of Nature
levelled at the point
by our greatness and our meanness.
And when our day is dawn
six feet deep in the womb
of the immense earth
in which we shall all go, carrying nothing.

I hail therefore, aged Master Senghor,
the intellectualman and democrat,
a man of conscience, that wisely reveres Truth.
Ancestor Nyerere sat in the shrine of Ujamaa
Sharing palm wine and colanuts.
He saw Truth in a dream and befriended it,

now his mind rests in peace, so shall his soul.
I laud King Mandela, Afrik's primal sample;
he gave it all to men
and had naught in his bag but Truth.
Now his mind is harmony, and with his soul.

As the sea begins to calm
the fumes of rushing streams,
and the rains subdue the rising dust
onto its mother earth,
clouds begin to clear on the skies of Africa
and Nature's will, will be done.

To the Proprietors of the Republic

I am no scab, no wag either
only a fated traveler groping
the pitch-dark night
for a grave to lay down my head

to lay down my head
in a grave and sleep in peace
so no rain drops in my ears
no horrors strain my troubled sight
no flies buzz about my feeble trunk
and keep me awake again

keep me awake again
to raise the splint that critics set ablaze
to hoist the monarchs in their gambling fits
divulge their shame
in the eyes of the world

in the eyes of the world I shall not flay
their shameless guilt
for, I am only a withered leaf
fluttering from my stalk in the gentle breeze
into a quiet grave to lay down my head
and sleep in peace.

In Memory of Dr Philip Agendia

A savage tale no tongue could tell
fell from the cracks of
dark Sunday morning
"Agendia is dead and gone"
crushed on the tarmac of an ill-fated day

Tall and sturdy, he was the robust dream
and the ebony art of Fuandem's hand
the meaning
of his life was putting meaning
in the lives of others

I mourn a friend
I mourn a friend who was more than a friend
a youthful guru
snatched from the steaming breast of life
and only his works remain
to mourn the living.

Lac Municipal

I long to swim out of the lake
where stands the still morbid swamps
where drunkards purge crammed bowels
where street dames hurl unripe births
where assassins rinse treacherous knives

I long to come away from the lake
and sail to the foot of Lebialem Falls
there I'll sit on a mighty rock
and listen to the ceaseless melody of
the tireless drumbeats of the waterfall

I'll sail away, sail away to Lebialem Falls
and dance and whirl and jump and sing
and hail the squirrels and the crows

joining in the ecstasy of the splash of golden
bubbles rumbling down from highest heights

I'll sit on the mightiest rock and watch
the kite stoop to the sunbird and the sparrow
lord the parrot and we shall sing and dance
and jaunt as the sweet foams of the golden falls
rise to caress the endless sky.

My Clansman's Benevolence

When the raiders came and went
I saw freedom knocking at our door
Knocking on the door of Africa

I woke up from a drowsy snooze
To hug my clansman in delight
In our gardens where love was sown

But he raised his shoulders like a cock
At wrestling and galled my bitter soul
With hatred, pride, and repression.

The Bigman's Son

I was hurrying through a stiff cold street
by villas planted on scarce-trodden greens
hemmed in firm iron bars
and I saw an handsome lad
lean wearily on the adamant gate
while monstrous hounds
growled hard at me.

Out of a window a damsel plunged her head
and saw her little lad glaring stern at me
a voice that almost wept railed from her heart:
"Ngwep ngwi, what are you doing there?
Come back home my all!"

42

and the rake-like housemaid
came panting after him
and the youngster turned
and sighed and said:

"Mother, let me out to feel the world
like that man walking as he likes"

As I traced my path away
I heard the youngman's plea
echoing in my restless brain
what a sigh I heaved for him
knowing that
the healthiest rose grows in the wild
where *ngwep ngwi* wants to
feel the world.

On the Departure of Haifa

The sap of the *ngongo* leaves
Stretched out green
in the evanescence of the year
And crabs that yawned at noontime
Found reason for their joy
In the clay beddable pond
Where only fresh *nkeng* saps
Stood waving bye to one
Who eclipsed my soul with a smile
At San Francisco Bay.

Njisoo

Set me down
Set me down
The burden is heavy to lift from my head

Where is Njisoo
With the magic wand of the other world

So wild
So fierce
The distant day in a little world so harsh with pain

On my head
They set their
Loads and strut with ease to the empire of the dead

But me
Weary
I limp, I toddle, I cry "set me down, set me down"

But
Where is Njisoo
Of the gloried days?

Conscience and the Man

Conscience:

"Why sit in the curtained Hall
Weeping with applause
What others can afford
Of an endearing endeavour?
Have you not quaffed enough
Of that wisdom that men of genius
Have on their admirers' feet displayed?
Why sit still quaffing the stuff
When with natures plumes and ink
All mankind can in the book of Fame
Their names inscribe?"

The Man:

"Many a man have passed by me
On the stony path
In a thorny forest
and asked
What good I was in the universe
With shame, I've hid my face

44

In the dark of day and yet asked
The meaning of my life."

Conscience:

"The meaning of life is putting
Meaning in your life"

The Man:

"I'm resolved, that of all the ink
That spits from the tongue of poetry
I shall display the beauty of my troubles
In the eyes of the world."

A Phantom in Heaven

I saw a phantom in heaven
When Fuandem blew his winding horn
And in swaddling ganduras the angels
Dropped from the heavy clouds and squatted
On his feet – I saw the little man
I saw him in another world when I was young
He sank his claws in my throat
Till I cried out in my dream
And woke God in His sleep.

City Woman

The long dreary day
wearies her out

yawning at the balcony
splitting hairs
painting nails
gazing at the clouds
wondering why they were clouds

waiting for a guest
hoping to be a bride
dreaming of a honeymoon

till darkness veils the day
and she searches in and out
for a bed beneath
a reckless drunken lout
for exchange of amorous gifts
of VDs and HIV-AIDS.

To a Shy Lad

Brave lad, be brave
Dress not cowardice your grave
Though the burning embers
In your chest yearn for human lust

Look deep in a lady's craving eyes
And climb to the world's
Imagined heights
Or lose the succulent world for fright

Brave lad, be brave…
Clothe not youth your cowardice
For if you do not spread out
Your arms in quest

You'd never know how rich or poor
Are the harvests of your embrace.

Buea Mountain

Piercing into the sky's heart
The monstrous wall spreads
Like a barricade
Sinking into Limbe Sea
Against the ugliness of the worlds

The huge red sun
Resting on its shoulders
Waits for a red man's sacrifice
Under the stubborn showers
With the blessing of the gods

Or the milky clouds
Watching from the giant's peak
Descend pitifully
On the tired conurbation

Of rusty corrugated sheets
Of crude dark stark staring stones
Of volcanic voluptuous vomit
Of life imprisoned in the idea
Of long abandoned dreams
Of falsehoods and banalities
Of bilingual brotherhood.

The Beauty of Life

If pain is the beauty of life
Then men must adore
For Joy is a dinosaur rare
A painted thing
An image in the clouds
A wink of sleep

If love be the beauty of life
Then men must love pain
For hatred abounds
And love is hard to find

If beauty is the object of life
Then men must love death
Because we live in death
And die in life
For Joy is a dinosaur rare.

A Gap in Her Teeth

Two rows of
milk-white teeth
ranged like marble
at the entrance
of Fuandem's shrine.
Hemmed by ebony lips
like the skin of gold
above all poetry
above all wisdom....

Peering through the crack
I see Bliss seated at akimbo.
Her smile
that was the charm of the gods
spread eternity at my feet.

Plastic Love

The horror
In the sensual sweet
Now
Separated from paradise
By a thin layer of the condom

If the riotous passion
Shall not yield to
The warm sensation of genuine love
Nay, let me play the eunuch
And dream till I am weary

Feel without being felt
Than being felt without the feel
Is plastic love

Nay let me stay, nay abstain
And dream like a eunuch
Till I am weary of life and death.
If true love I shall not find.

Letters to Marion
(And the Coming Generations)

1

One savage night of lust
breathes in a nose flesh and blood
the morning wakes
and 'Hallelujah' is the song of joy
and innocence writhing in her cot
begins a trek of passion grief and gloom
along the labyrinths of time.

2

is there any comfort in what one loves
if he found it hidden in a cloak?

the cat is a stealthier philosopher and
cries not when the owl scares the night
with ominous songs
there is comelier evil
in the smiles of handsome men
now that we must go to church to serve the devil
now that the party and partymen
must send politic winds on treetops
whose leaves are shed
now that our indignity must
run fierce fevers in every nerve

the cry of the owl has gone too wild, too long
since Wandji, Wambo, Nyobe,
Moumie, Jua... went abroad
with blisters from tyrants' knives
and when our morning wakes
our stalls are empty
our history's eclipsed in the fists of power
and our fields littered with lives
that had known life

is there any comfort knowing the fate
of a little girl writhing in her cot?

3

I mock civilisations and spit
in the face of Africa's independence
life was not stone-breaking
till the empire was auctioned
for toy crowns
those men were born when God was asleep
they have never found peace in their graves.

4

there's an image torments my sleep
the land of prawns will know more plagues
till the old men, their souls shall find
a resting place
and their blood smeared in the clan's shrine

as I speak
ghosts in a troubled mirror
laugh some weird laughter
and a sudden flood of blood
high like Mount Fako surges on
from the mouth of the Mungo
and everywhere agony shrieks.

5

Now's the time to read my will...

Children of, Cameroon, children of Africa
Love your trades
find fortune in imagination
and bring the souls of men to life
bring the lives of men to God
find Fuandem askew in the nave
and drink from springs that flow uphill.

no more of the Mungo's salty paste
where shabby politicmen wash their wounds
shame has chilled them to the bone
because they put honour in an empty song
and shed few tears when history climbers fell

no marbled mansions, no mammon piles
the silver spoon, the golden beads
these you shall not aspire
a savage night has dulled their lustre
and all civilisations have come to naught
if they meant bitterer days and nights

No, Marion, shed no tear
nor walk on broken dreams
stow away your prodigal soul
from shallow ponds
that drowned men's lives
and I drowned:

turn to the gem of tradition
turn to ancestral laws of right and wrong
and find therein some hope
some life that's worth the life

an ancestor knew the cult -
he lies beneath a cliff
near the palace walls
under a grassy mound
no memory living passed by unsighing

send imagination among those hills
where valleys heap beyond valleys
and find the hidden thing in the heart of
the universe

6

there in the armpit of the cliff
in ancestral rank
the poet and Messenger be laid.
on the tombstone
these words are cut
by friends who saw an image in a dream:

> *Here dead*
> *Lies life*
> *Go gently by.*

The Beginning

I was born to be a student grave
To climb the greasy mountains brave
Thrust myself in the trembling noise
Of Nature's wholesome voice.
For five long years, I went away from home
To Seat of Wisdom College, sacred intellect dome
I bade goodbye to young and old
To a land of the sage no one ever told
Cronies in tears shook faint my hand
And wished me good luck over the land
My box being light, I walked but fast
At four by day was I in school at last
Nineteen Seventy one, liberation year
From dad and mum like the youthful seer
Now all my rank were presented
But I felt so isolated and resented
Nor name nor person did I know nor seek
With smiles like such on a mermaids' cheek
And walked so freely to dorm Reverend
As though Sept would never have an end
But night came with horror on its throne
And all in the Ref were flung as thrown
With appetizing taste and scraping plate
A new-won friend was father of his fate
We told ourselves tales of blissful kind
Most from Imagination, sacred priest of mankind
Each would tell his experience through
How the devil led him to the grave in a bough
And bade him be a footballer all his life
How he watched fights in films 'tween man and wife
Of guerillas, of monsters, wizards eating men
Frightened thus we sought our beds to pray amen
How I slept, nay, dreamed beyond dream
And the face of things in the earth was dim
Till the sun with courage shamed the moon
And all my dreams were buried at noon

Pleasures continue with great delight
And three days ere our signors come with spite
Three days we were told our merriment lasts
For signors came with torments and bullying blasts
Being small, some thought I came for escort
But eyes that swallowed me could not retort
For, often as I walked around and made them know
Made them know I was a scholar. Some said "no"
Hands to mouth, others chilled with awe and wonder
Exclaiming, "The midget, true he's a scholar!"
In language metaphorical they named me "Government
Height", loved me well like nurses well-meant
As days passed fast I was like a suckling
baby to them all. Could I to them forever cling
When every minute's tick sent my nurses home
Forsaking me alone in the intellect-dome
I sang farewell in song and sorrow
scathed like the shaft of the poisoned arrow

The year ended, change and stuff did come
And "Semi-Fox" so they called, I had become
With torments, tortures greatly much reduced
Vantage fed me more than preps, as I induced
Risks came much more when I reached Form Three
And I was poised like Eve for the Knowledge Tree
Many tricks played on me, O, I was beguiled
And man I was to fight those who me belied
Success brought the third year home, I was proud
Up and down the holiday town wore a clam'rous shroud
Of students talking wondrously of school life
Many I knew, always loved to blow their fife
But I held with me my "Abott" very much conceited
Up and down the clam'rous town as though initiated
Doctor in some Aristotle or hackneyed-teeth Plato
Or some wild and uncanny memento
Fate wished me luck, sometimes ill luck
And my fortune was stowed in stock and lock
For when devil thunder came with wily smiles
I saw my life in patio of distant miles
And to fourth year I climbed on a greasy pole
Like a semi-finalist in a football pool

Counting but days to the crest of life
That is to say, to reach form five
But thunder threatened devastation
I welcomed it with woe and station
The ever-guiding Monarch calm and canny
And whose fortune was so bright and sunny
In whose superintendence I threw my lot in full
And climbed the heights, not like the French fool
Who in a thousand years climbed the Alps
And in one woeful day fell in the fatal laps
Of indignant mother Earth. I climbed the heights

I climbed the heights in my intellectual fights
Till I saw the final days drifting me home
I knew I had done all to reach the final dome
Where learned men like saints adorn the painted walls
For an intellectual man is a fetish man in the halls
Of profane ignorance; a man of learning's a holy man
He is procurer of all that in life is death and human
But thoughts of my destiny when after school
Would make me gnash my teeth, go to pee and stool
Now unaided a man shall work and toil and sweat
Hope, hope till all his hopes are dry and wet
Now is time to feed one's thoughts with nostalgia
Cry for the day father clothed our lives with regalia
But truth is that success anoints all brows
Of he that works hard and to blind Fortune bows
I shall tell myself this tale without offence
As now full grieved with joy I leave from thence

Adieu, the sanctified sacred shrine of knowledge
Adieu, Our Lady Seat of Wisdom College
I go into the world with your blessings as a sage.